I didn't know that people chase twisters

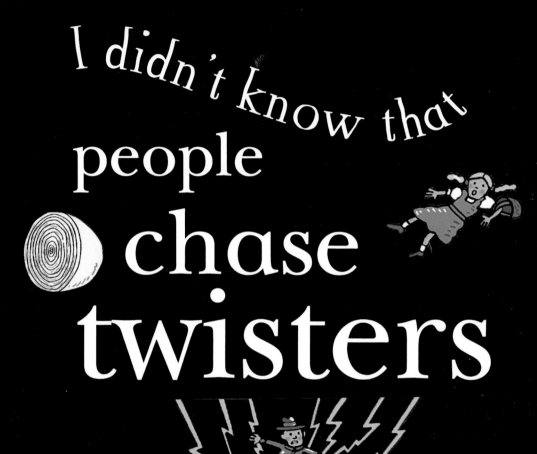

© Aladdin Books Ltd 1998
© U.S. text 1998
Produced by
Aladdin Books Ltd
28 Percy Street
London W1P 0LD

First published in the United States in 1998 by
Copper Beech Books,
an imprint of
The Millbrook Press
2 Old New Milford Road
Brookfield, Connecticut 06804

Concept, editorial, and design by
David West Children's Book Design

Illustrators: Peter Roberts and Jo Moore

Printed in Belgium

Library of Congress Cataloging-in-Publication Data
Petty, Kate.
People chase twisters : and other amazing facts
about violent weather / by Kate Petty ;
illustrated by Peter Roberts and Jo Moore.
p. cm. — (I didn't know that—)
Includes index.
Summary: Provides information about violent weather phenomena such as
thunderstorms, lightning, blizzards, monsoons, and sandstorms.
ISBN 0-7613-0715-X (lib. bdg.). — ISBN 0-7613-0647-1 (trade : hc)
1. Storms—Juvenile literature. 2. Weather—Juvenile literature.
[1. Storms. 2. Weather.] I. Roberts, Peter, 1925- ill. II. Moore, Jo, ill.
III. Title. IV. Series.
QC941.3.P48 1998   97-41607
551.55—dc21   CIP AC
5 4 3 2 1

I didn't know that people chase twisters

Kate Petty

COPPER BEECH BOOKS
BROOKFIELD, CONNECTICUT

I didn't know that

Introduction

Did *you* know that dust devils can be a half mile high? ... that hurricanes can pile up boats like bath toys? ... that it can rain frogs, fish, and children?

Discover for yourself amazing facts about violent weather, from the hailstone as big as a tennis ball (but much heavier!) to the storm surge that can fling boats a half mile inland.

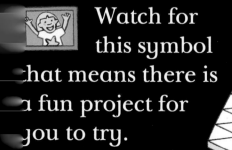

Watch for this symbol that means there is a fun project for you to try.

Is it true or is it false? Watch for this symbol and try to answer the question before reading on for the answer.

I didn't know that

you can float up and down in clouds. William Rankin did when he bailed out of his plane in a violent thunderstorm. He was bounced around in the clouds, battered by the wind, for a terrifying 40 minutes before finally parachuting to safety.

In 1876, Denonath Sircar of Bangladesh clung to a broken branch all night to save himself in a flood that washed away millions of homes.

The terrible hurricane that hit the Caribbean in 1780 killed 20,000 people. The wind was so violent that it hurled a 12-pound cannon 420 feet.

In 1931, a Minnesota tornado tossed a railroad car 82 feet through the air.

Deanna Wyant and her boyfriend actually flew around the room when a tornado hit their apartment in 1965. The building collapsed but miraculously they both survived!

I didn't know that

thunderheads can be over nine miles high. The name for a thundercloud is cumulonimbus. Cumulus means "heaped" and nimbus means "rain cloud." You can see fluffy, low-level cumulus clouds building up into tall thunderclouds in warm weather.

 Leave an upturned jar on a saucer of water in a sunny spot for an hour. The heat of the sun will cause some of the water to *evaporate* and rise as invisible water vapor. Watch the *condensation* forming on the glass as the invisible water vapor cools and it starts to "rain."

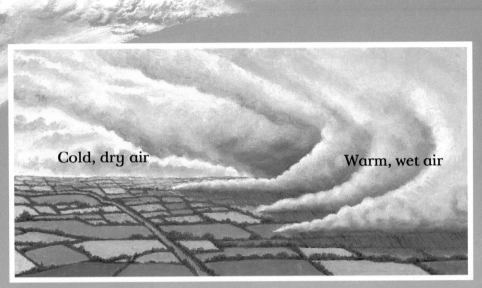

Cold, dry air

Warm, wet air

Clouds can be formed in many ways. In this case, a warm air mass moves in from the right. It rises over cold air moving in from the left. Rain forms where the masses meet.

3 The base of the cloud is low. The top is very high.

2 The air cools as it gets higher and droplets form.

1 In hot weather warm, wet air and dust rise to form cumulus clouds.

Around the Equator there are about 30,000 thunderstorms every day.

ONE AND TWO AND THREE AND

I didn't know that

thunder is the sound of lightning. The moving air inside a thundercloud builds up *static electricity*. This causes a huge flash of lightning that heats the air to 18,000°F. The air expands and explodes, making a thunderclap.

How far away is the storm? Count the seconds between the time when you see the lightning and the time when you hear the thunder. Count a half mile for every three seconds.

In 1778, trendy Parisian ladies wore lightning conductors on their hats.

Don't try Benjamin Franklin's famous 1752 experiment with a kite and a key to prove the electrical nature of lightning. A Swedish scientist, trying it out for himself in 1909, was electrocuted.

Reports of "ball lightning" have not been scientifically proved. A ball of lightning supposedly floated around a hotel room in France before drifting out of the window and exploding nearby.

In 1894, a hailstone that landed in the U.S. contained a frozen turtle.

 True or false?
Firing shells at clouds can prevent hailstorms.

Answer: **True**
Anti-hail gunners in Uzbekistan fire shells, scattering tiny particles into the clouds. The smaller hailstones that cling to them melt before reaching the ground.

The largest *hailstones* fell during a storm in Bangladesh that killed 92 people in 1986. Each hailstone weighed up to two pounds.

I didn't know that

some hailstones are the size of tennis balls. In India, these huge hailstones smashed car windshields, flattened crops, and killed thousands of birds. Many farmers now insure themselves against hail damage.

Can you find the fish?

A hailstone has layers, like an onion. It picks up a layer of ice each time it goes up and down in the thundercloud.

I didn't know that

people lie down in a blizzard. This is a good survival tip as the blanket of snow traps a layer of warm air around the body. Remember to make an airhole! Animals often survive in the snow this way.

SEARCH & FIND SEARCH & FIND & SEARCH
Can you find the backpack?

Snowflakes form when water vapor rapidly freezes as crystals around dust particles. Each snow crystal has six sides and each one is unique. Catch some on a dark glove and study them (quickly!) through a magnifying glass.

In 1978, 27 inches of snow fell on Boston in 24 hours.

Avalanche! A weakness in a layer of snow on a slope or a precipice can start an avalanche. As thousands of tons of snow roars downhill, it can reach speeds of over 186 mph, burying everything in its path.

St. Bernard dogs were first kept by monks in the Swiss mountains to rescue people trapped in the snow. They wore barrels of brandy for reviving the patients.

I didn't know that

a *monsoon* can last for up to six months. Water from the Indian Ocean evaporates in the winter and then falls as torrential rain in the summer monsoons. Farmers in low-lying parts of India can lose everything. In July, Bombay, India, has eight times as much rain as New York!

Showers of frogs have occurred in many places such as India and England! Other showers include crabs, fish, and jellyfish.

 You can make your own rain gauge from a flat-bottomed plastic bottle. Find out how much rain falls in July where you live.

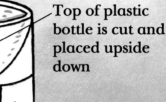

Top of plastic bottle is cut and placed upside down

Measure in inches

Bottom filled with water to point where measure starts

Land is flooded when rain makes a river rise over its banks. Noah's flood is based on fact. There were floods in the Tigris-Euphrates valley in Turkey and Mesopotamia around 4000 B.C.

I didn't know that

hurricanes have eyes. The *currents of air* in a hurricane spiral upward to form a rotating circle of wind around a central "chimney." This calm center is called the "eye."

SEARCH & FIND Can you find the satellite? FIND & SEARCH

Eye

Winds over 186 mph can cause unimaginable destruction. In 1992, Hurricane Andrew hit an area south of Florida, tearing roofs and walls off houses, smashing trees and cars, and piling up boats like little plastic toys!

 True or false?

Hurricanes are given girls' and boys' names.

Answer: **True**
Atlantic hurricanes are given alternate girls' and boys' names in alphabetical order from the beginning of the season. This makes them easier to identify.

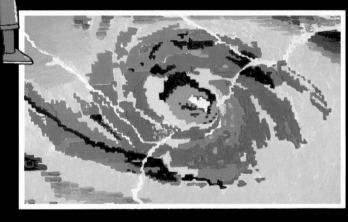

Infra-red pictures from satellites provide color-coded information about tropical storms. Scientists can track their progress and warn people in time.

Hurricane Andrew caused $46.5 billion worth of damage.

Even a warship such as an aircraft carrier can crumple like tin in a typhoon. This is what happened to *U.S.S. Hornet* near Okinawa, Japan, in 1945.

I didn't know that

typhoons can sink ships. *Tropical storms* can whip up mountainous waves. The highest wave ever measured was 85 feet, but the highest ever seen was 111 feet. Ships are helpless in such stormy seas.

20

True or false?

Hurricanes, tropical cyclones, and typhoons are all the same thing.

Answer: **True**

Tropical storms are called hurricanes in the Atlantic Ocean, cyclones in the Indian Ocean, typhoons in the China Sea, and willy-willies in Australia.

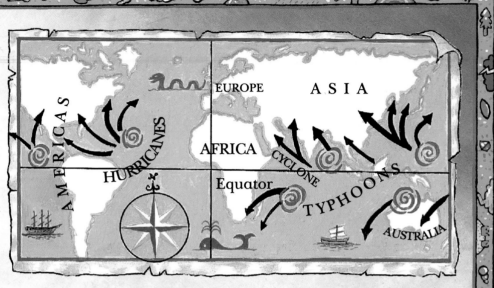

A *storm surge* carried this boat nearly a half mile inland. Huge waves can surge in ahead of a hurricane, flooding low-lying areas.

"Raining" fish are sucked up and carried far away before falling.

I didn't know that
tornadoes can make children fly.

Tornadoes are like small, ferocious storms. People, animals, and whole houses can be picked up and dropped some distance away. In 1986, thirteen Chinese schoolchildren were carried 12 miles by a tornado before being deposited completely unharmed!

A dust devil in the desert is a miniature tornado. Spinning winds whirl sand and dust to heights of between 300–3,000 feet.

Can you find 13 children?

SEARCH & FIND & SEARCH & FIND

A whirling cloud turns into a waterspout as water is sucked up. It is spectacular, but not terribly dangerous.

A tornado, or "twister," comes down out of thunder-clouds like an "elephant's trunk," a spinning funnel of cloud that sucks up dust and soil. The funnel gets tighter and the wind gets faster, up to 500 mph.

! Some tornadoes are born in hurricanes.

I didn't know that

people chase twisters. The more people understand about tornadoes, the easier it will be to predict when one is coming along. Scientists study tornadoes by following them and putting monitoring equipment in their path to assess their strength.

Tornadoes sometimes appear in pairs. These pairs are called "sisters."

24

An eyewitness described a tornado in 1928: "The great shaggy end of the funnel hung directly overhead. There was a strong gassy odor. The walls were of rotating clouds with constant flashes of lightning that zigzagged from side to side."

 True or false?

People can make their own twisters.

Answer: **True**

But not full-size ones! Japanese scientist Tetsuya Fujita studies miniature tornadoes made of dry ice.

In 24 hours, 148 tornadoes blew in the southern and midwestern U.S.

I didn't know that

sandstorms can strip paint off a car. Loose dust and sand in deserts can easily be whipped up by the wind, flinging millions of stinging grains at every surface. Sand-carrying winds carve desert rocks into strange shapes.

Industrial sand-blasting is used to strip dirt and paint off old buildings to make them look new again.

Sand-carved rock found in the desert

A terrifying 9,000-foot-high storm turns the sky dark and sandblasts everything in its path.

True or false?

The Sahara has always been a desert.

Answer: **False**

Climate can change. Cave paintings in the Sahara show that it was once home to all types of animals that could only live where there was water and grass.

There were dust storms in the American midwest in the 1930s. The rain failed and wind blew the dry soil around. Farmers couldn't grow anything, so people starved.

I didn't know that

weather forecasters use information from space. Satellites high above the Earth send back pictures of cloud movements. They show where storms are brewing.

This scientist fires a rocket into thunder-clouds. Wires attached to the rocket trigger a charge of lightning.

Weather balloons, called radiosondes, can record and transmit weather conditions as they travel upward.

Weather stations all over the world take temperature, wind, rain, and *air pressure* readings and feed them into computers.

 Be a weather observer yourself. Record your observations at the same time every day. You will need a thermometer, a rain gauge (see p.17), a weather vane nearby, and a copy of the *Beaufort scale* for describing the strength of the wind.

HURRICANE GILBERT

JULY day	date	🌡	💧	🌀	🚩	
Mon	1	75	1"	SW	light	overcast heavy rain
Tues	2					
Wed	3					
Thurs	4					
Fri	5					
Sat	6					
Sun	7					

Meteorology comes from Greek and means "thing in the heaven above."

Glossary

Air pressure
The weight of the air pressing down on the land. High pressure usually means good weather and low pressure usually means bad weather.

Avalanche
Rush of snow down a mountainside.

Beaufort scale
An illustrated scale measuring the force of the wind from calm to hurricane.

Climate
The sort of weather a particular place has come to expect over a long time.

Condensation
This happens when a gas, such as water vapor, cools to form droplets of liquid. Clouds are formed this way with droplets of water.

Currents of air
Stream of moving air.

Evaporation
This happens when a liquid, such as water, is heated and turns into a gas that rises into the air.

Hailstones
Pieces of ice, formed in thunderclouds, that fall to the ground, often in warm weather.

Infra-red

Satellites can use infra-red rays to show the different heat patterns as pictures – clouds show up as bright (cold) and deserts as dark (hot).

Storm surge

Waves blown before the wind that can cause flooding, especially if forced through a narrow channel.

Monsoon

The name of the south-westerly wind that brings heavy rain to parts of Asia in the summer; also the name given to the rainy season in those places.

Tropical storms

Violent storms that develop in the hot (over 80° F), moist air above warm seas near the Equator in summer and fall.

Static electricity

Electricity that isn't flowing in a current. It builds up from friction (such as when you rub a balloon or stroke a cat), or from lots of activity in a cloud.

Index

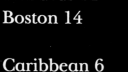
 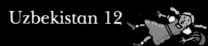